GW01459098

When Somebod,

Sheila Hollins, Sandra Dowling and Noëlle Blackman
illustrated by Catherine Brighton

Beyond Words

London

EALING LIBRARIES www.ealing.gov.uk

91400000283288

5

13

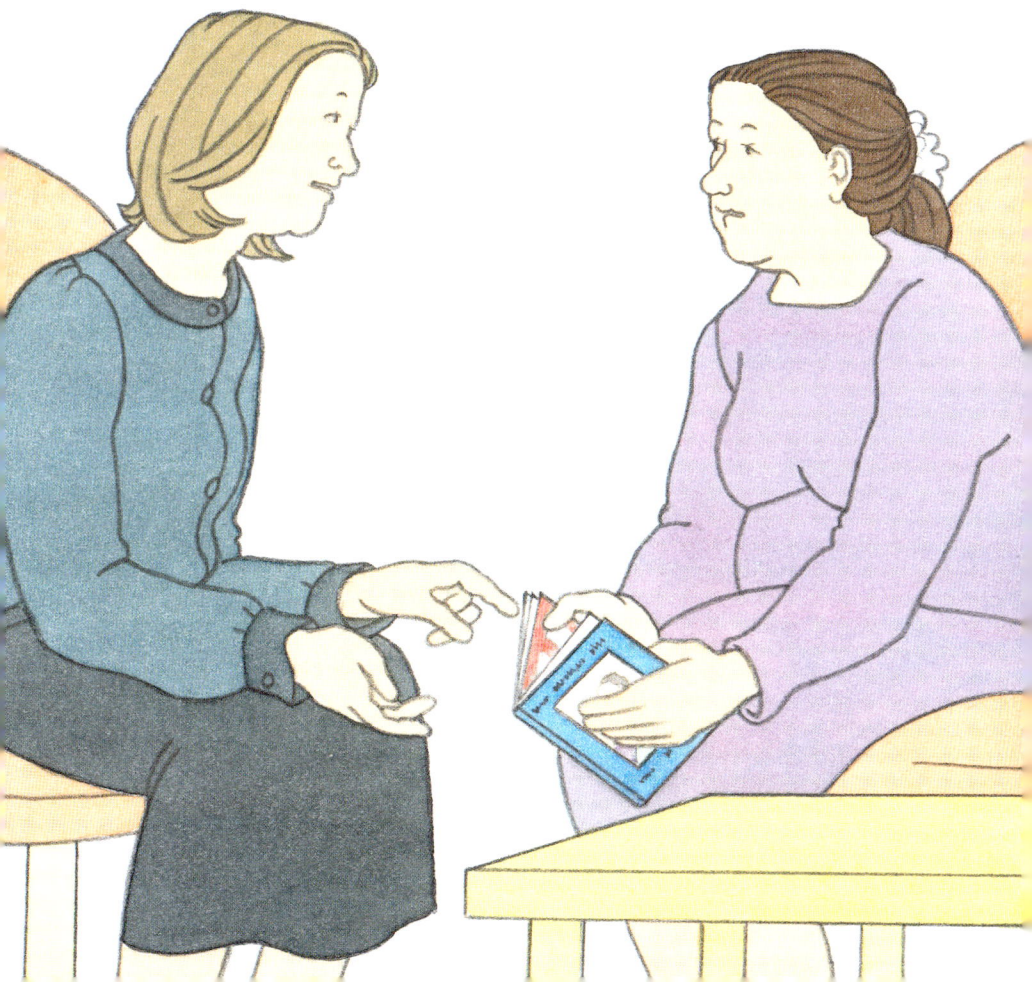

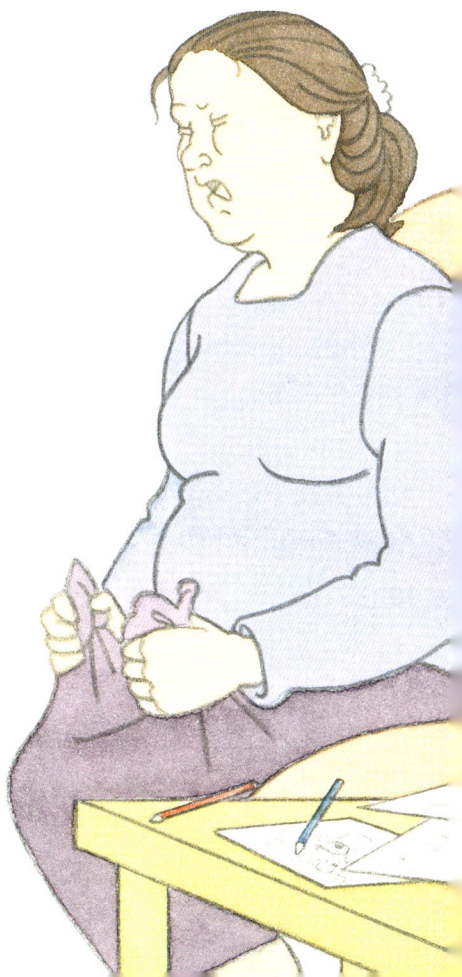

22

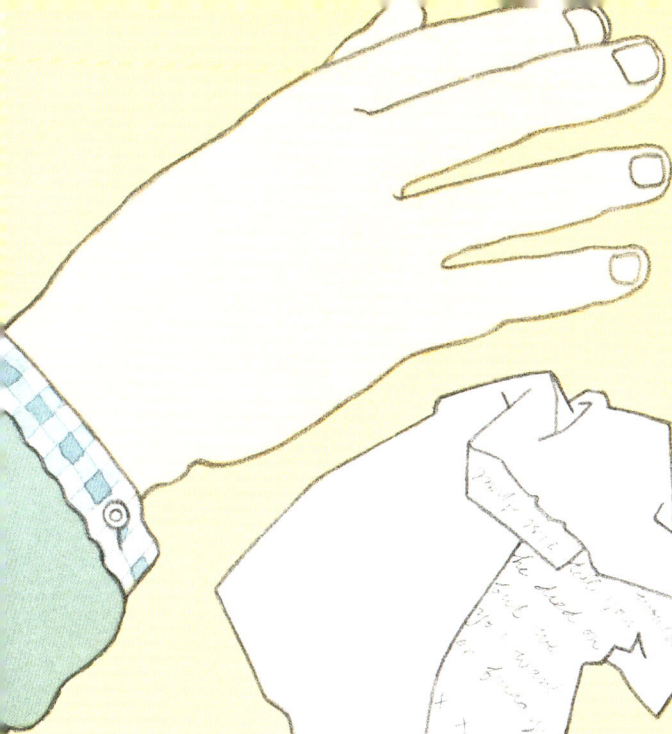

36

First published in the UK 2003 by Gaskell and St George's Hospital Medical School.

This edition published 2014 by Books Beyond Words.

Text & illustrations © Sheila Hollins & Catherine Brighton 2014.

No part of this book may be reproduced in any form, or by any means without the prior permission in writing from the publisher.

ISBN 978-1-78458-003-2

British Library Cataloguing-in-Publication Data
A catalogue record for this book is available from the British Library.

Printed by DX Imaging, Watford.

Books Beyond Words is a Community Interest Company registered in England and Wales (7557861).

St George's Hospital Charity is a registered charity (no. 241527).

Contents

The following words are provided for people who want a ready-made story rather than tell their own.

1.   Mary and Frank have been to a funeral. They both look very upset.

2.   On the way home they meet the postman and a neighbour. Frank says hello. Mary looks away. She is feeling sad.

3.   Mary and Frank are sitting on the sofa. There are lots of photographs of family and friends on the cupboard. Frank is watching TV. Mary is thinking. The cat is sleeping on her knee.

4.   Mary is crying. She is on her own in the kitchen. She is holding a photograph. Perhaps she misses the person in the picture.

5.   Frank tries to comfort Mary but she turns away. She holds the picture close to her.

6.   Frank hides the picture from Mary. He thinks this will help because Mary gets upset when she looks at it. Mary sees him from the door.

7.   Mary is cross. She comes into the room and shouts at Frank. She yells, "Leave the picture alone!" Frank doesn't know what to say.

8.   Frank leaves the room. Mary is alone. She is thinking about the person in the picture.

9.   Frank meets a friend in the café. Perhaps he can help.

10. Frank tells his friend that Mary is sad because someone has died. He says he wants to help but doesn't know how. Frank's friend listens carefully.

11. Frank brings a pizza home. He wants to cheer Mary up.

12. Mary and Frank enjoy the pizza. Mary is looking a little better. She is glad that Frank is trying to help her.

13. Mary doesn't want to go to the café. She is worried but Frank says, "You will be OK."

14. Mary, Frank and their friend talk about how Mary is feeling.

15. Mary tells their friend that someone she loves has died. He has an idea about what might help.

16. The friend telephones a bereavement counsellor. He makes an appointment for Mary.

17a. Mary's friend takes her to meet the counsellor.

17. Mary meets the counsellor. She seems very nice.

18. The counsellor explains how she can help. Mary can tell the counsellor about how she feels. The counsellor will listen to Mary, and help her to remember the person who has died.

19a. Mary visits the counsellor again.

19. Mary cries. The counsellor understands. She lets Mary cry. This helps her to feel better.

20a. Mary arrives for her counselling appointment.

20. Mary brings some photographs to show to the counsellor. She is talking about her memories. Mary says she misses the person who died.

21a. Mary has come for counselling again. It is winter now. She has been coming since the summertime.

21. The counsellor listens to what Mary says. She really understands.

22. Mary goes to the grave with the counsellor. She has brought some flowers. She wants to put the flowers on the grave.

23. Mary is feeling much better now. She is at home with Frank having breakfast. He is glad that Mary feels better.

24. The postman brings a letter for Frank.

25 Frank opens his letter. It is bad news. Frank is shocked.

26. Frank crushes the letter. He drops it. A photograph falls out.

27. Frank shows the photograph to Mary. She puts her arm around him. She knows how it feels when someone dies. Mary comforts Frank.

28. Frank is alone. He is looking out of the window. He is holding the photograph in his hand. He looks sad.

29. Frank and Mary look through this book together. Mary is helping Frank by talking to him and comforting him.

30. Mary and Frank go to the funeral together. Frank's friends are there too.

31. Mary, Frank and his friends are together. They are talking about the person who has died. They know how to help each other. They are trying to support one another.

32. Mary and Frank leave to go home. They both look sad. Perhaps it reminds Mary of her own bereavement.

33. Mary and Frank put photographs into an album. These will help them to remember the people who have died.

34. Frank is feeling a little better. He has done some shopping. He talks to his neighbour on the way home.

35. Frank sees Mary in the café talking to their friend.

36. Frank decides to join Mary and their friend. Mary and Frank look happy now.

What is grief?

When somebody dies we experience many different emotions. Sometimes people say they feel numb and helpless. They may be shocked and overwhelmed by the news. Often it is difficult to take in what has happened; "I just can't believe it," some may say over and over.

People may feel angry with doctors, nurses or carers. They may blame others for the death. They may also be angry with the person who has died, for leaving them. Some bereaved people feel guilty, or regretful about things that happened before the death. People often say they feel overwhelmingly sad. They may yearn for their loved ones or even search for them, half-expecting to see them again. People may become withdrawn, or have difficulty sleeping or finding peace of mind during the day. This is grief.

People grieve in different ways. Every society and culture has its own way of dealing with death. It is important to be familiar with rituals which are relevant locally.

While some of our grief is shared with other people, other aspects are more personal. Commonly, people will visit the grave of their loved one, or the site where ashes were placed. There may be days when memories are especially acute such as birthdays or other special anniversaries.

Listening to music, visiting a favourite place, or taking up activities enjoyed by the person who has died, are just some ways that help people to remember and to grieve. Some people think that death changes a relationship rather than ends it. They may continue to talk to their friend or relative while looking at a photograph or by the grave. They may say things they wish had been said before the death, or simply tell the person who has died about everyday happenings. Others may write letters or a journal as a way of maintaining a bond. For some people, this can be very comforting and an important part of their personal grieving.

What happens to people with learning disabilities when somebody dies?

It is sometimes hard to describe our feelings to other people, especially as they do not always know what to do or say to help. For someone with a learning disability this can be even more difficult. One thing that adds to this difficulty is the attitude of society. For instance, in the past many people with learning disabilities were not told when someone died. It was often thought that they would not understand or that they would get too upset. We know now that it is better to tell people if someone dies. It is vital to be sensitive to people's feelings when telling bad news and it should be done by someone who knows them well.

People are likely to be upset when they hear that someone they love has died. This is perfectly natural and should not be ignored or stifled.

Inclusion is important, not just immediately after the death, but in the following months and years. Many people with learning disabilities do not have the opportunity to grieve in a personal way. They may never have gone to visit the cemetery, but when given the chance many are keen to do so.

Often people do not have any mementos or even photographs to help them to remember. Some people's memories may be sketchy, and if details have not been recorded, their pasts may be unknown to the people who know them now.

Remembering is an important part of grieving, so it is vital that memories are available to people with learning disabilities. Life-story books, memory boxes or a family tree are useful ways of recording a person's life history in a way that is accessible. This may help people not only to cope with death but also to enjoy life.

If people are not given the chance to be involved in the collective activities of grief, or they are not supported to grieve in a personal way, it can become difficult for them to find ways to understand their loss.

People may not have had the chance to learn ways to express their feelings. By being kept away from funerals, wakes or other rituals and by not sharing in the feelings of their grieving relatives, many will have missed out on the opportunity to learn how others behave, in their cultural setting, following a death.

We all learn how to play our part from watching others, but people with learning disabilities are somehow expected to know what happens, without having had the chance to learn. Some people find it hard to communicate their thoughts and ideas to others, and it may also be hard for them to understand what others tell them.

It is important that carers, family members and friends talk to bereaved people about what has happened and how they are feeling, and that they try to find out what they can do to help. This may only mean taking a little extra time and care, and being aware of the bereaved person's feelings.

Grief can last for a long time, several months or several years. This depends on the nature of the loss and on individual responses to it.

No one should be expected to feel 'better' after just a few weeks. Also, feelings of grief may subside for a time and then reappear later, and at such times particular care and understanding are needed.

Emotional distress may be shown through the way people behave. They may become withdrawn or agitated, they may be aggressive or unusually passive, or there may be other changes in the way they act. Others may not realise that these changes are related to their bereavement. They may be labelled as having 'challenging behaviour', and services may be designed around this label, while the loss and pain go unnoticed.

It is very important that carers, family members and friends are aware that changes in behaviour could be an expression of feelings, however recent or distant their loss.

Does bereavement counselling work with people with learning disabilities?

A research study, 'Bereavement interventions for people with learning disabilities' (Hollins, Hubert and Dowling, *Bereavement Care* 22, 2003) has tried to answer the question 'What helps a person with learning disabilities when someone close to them dies?'. The research found that counselling helps people to feel better. It was not enough to ask support workers and family carers to provide extra help and understanding.

Counselling someone with a learning disability

Many counsellors feel that they do not have the skills to work with someone who has a learning or communication disability, although those who have done so find that it is really very similar to counselling anyone else. Some adjustments to a counsellor's usual way of working may be needed when working with someone who has a learning disability, according to their individual needs. The following pages give some points to consider.

Communication

Find out about how a client prefers to communicate before you begin to work together. You could ask the client, or whoever referred them for counselling.

If the client has limited verbal communication skills, it may be helpful for someone who knows them well to accompany them to the sessions, to help you to understand one another. You may need to simplify your language and support what you say with signs and symbols, or to emphasise your facial expressions. If someone's speech is unclear you may find that it becomes easier to understand what the person is saying as time goes by.

Some people may say very little. They may be shy or think that no one is concerned with what they have to say. It might be unusual for someone else to be interested in their thoughts and feelings. It may, therefore, be difficult for people to tell you what they think or how they feel.

Their reticence does not necessarily mean that they do not understand what you are saying. Do continue to talk and share your thoughts and ideas. As you get to know one another it is likely that your client will be able to communicate more freely with you.

Think about offering a wide range of communication techniques. Drawing and painting can be a good way for people to 'say' how they are feeling. Puppets or dolls can help someone to tell a story or to express something difficult. Other pictures and photographs can also be useful to supplement the pictures in this book (see the list of books and packs that can help with communication). Remember that no single way will work with everybody.

People with learning disabilities, perhaps because of a desire to please or a fear of getting something wrong, may respond in the way they think you want them to. It is important to try to word questions impartially, and to be aware of any signals that may influence your client's reply.

Consent

It should never be assumed that people are not able to make their own decisions simply because they have a learning or communication disability. An investment in time and communication with the person concerned and his or her carers is necessary. Information should be given to people in a straightforward way, using plain language, visual prompts or pictures (as in this book), and signs and symbols as required.

For further information about consent, see *Reference guide to consent for examination or treatment* (Department of Health, 2009) and *Mental Capacity Act 2005 Code of Practice* (Ministry of Justice, 2007).

Few people understand what counselling will involve before they have experienced it. If the person comes to the session willingly, it will be very clear after an initial assessment whether they want to come again. Others will try it and see if they like it. If someone shows an unwillingness to continue with sessions, he or she should be supported to withdraw from counselling in an appropriate and sensitive manner.

Confidentiality

The confidentiality of the counselling situation is essentially the same when working with a client who has a learning or communication disability as when working with any other client. However, you may become worried that your client is ill, is at risk from someone else, or is a risk to themselves or someone else.

It is important to discuss issues of confidentiality with your client at the outset. You could say something like this: "I will not tell anyone else what we talk about in our sessions, unless you say something that makes me worried about you. If I need to tell anyone about something you have said, we will talk about the best way to do this. I will not say anything to other people that you do not know about." If you discuss your sessions with a supervisor, you should mention this to your client.

Useful resources

Where to find help and advice

Cruse Bereavement Care
Cruse is the national organisation for bereaved people. Some Cruse branches have bereavement supporters who work with people with learning disabilities. Cruse provides information about local bereavement counselling services and also gives welfare advice.
Helpline: 0844 477 9400
www.cruse.org.uk

Respond
Supports people with learning disabilities, their carers and professionals around any issue of trauma, including bereavement.
Helpline 0800 808 0700.
www.respond.org.uk

It is usually possible to access bereavement counselling through a GP, although this is often very short-term counselling. Many Community Learning Disability Teams (CLDTs) can offer bereavement counselling.

It is worth contacting local bereavement counselling services to find out whether they offer counselling to people with learning disabilities.

If they do not, this may be because they have never thought about it before. They may be prepared to, but may feel that they do not have enough knowledge. They might want to know more about what it means to have a learning disability and how they might need to extend their skills. They may decide that they would like to have some special training. This could be provided in a number of different ways:

- some advocacy and self-advocacy groups offer training about learning disability
- some Community Learning Disability Teams provide training
- the training could be provided by a specialist training service.

Since 2005, everyone in England who has a learning disability has been encouraged to have a health action plan. A bereavement need could be included in a person's health action plan, which would then mean that they should be supported to get any help they need in order to access bereavement counselling.

For more information about health action plans see *Action for Health – Health Action Plans and Health Facilitation*, which contains detailed good practice guidance. Available free from the Department of Health. An easy read version for people with learning disabilities is also available:
learning disabilitynurse.com/wp-content uploads/2012/02/health-action-plans1/pdf

Written information

Am I Allowed to Cry? A Study of Bereavement amongst People who have Learning Difficulties by Maureen Oswin. Souvenir Press, London.

Loss and Learning Disability by Noëlle Blackman. This book is for support workers, therapists and counsellors working with people with learning disabilities, showing how they can be affected by bereavement. It includes ways to prevent normal grief from becoming a bigger problem and to help people when the grief process 'goes wrong'. Worth Publishing, London.

How to Break Bad News to People with Intellectual Disabilities: A Guide for Carers and Professionals by Irene Tuffrey-Wijne. This book offers guidelines for practitioners to ease the process of breaking bad news, including news of a bereavement, to people with learning disabilities as sensitively and successfully as possible.

Easy Health (www.easyhealth.org.uk)
Provides a good range of easy read leaflets and other resources on health and wellbeing topics including grief.

Videos

Coping with Death. Explains what happens when somebody dies, and shows adults with learning disabilities coping with death. £30 (inc. p&p) from Speak Up Self Advocacy. The DVD can be ordered direct from the catalogue:
www.friendlyresource.org.uk.

Related titles in the Books Beyond Words series

When Mum Died (2014, 4th edition) by Sheila Hollins, and Lester Sireling, illustrated by Beth Webb. The story of a family dealing with the death of a parent told through pictures in a simple, honest and moving way. This book shows a burial.

When Dad Died (2014, 4th edition) by Sheila Hollins and Lester Sireling, illustrated by Beth Webb. A partner book to *When Mum Died*, showing a family dealing with the loss of a father. This book shows a cremation.

Am I Going to Die? (2009) by Sheila Hollins and Irene Tuffrey-Wijne, illustrated by Lisa Kopper. Tells the story of John, who has a terminal illness. It deals with physical deterioration and the emotional aspects of dying in an honest and moving way.

Getting On With Cancer (2002) by Veronica Donaghy, Jane Bernal, Irene Tuffrey-Wijne and Sheila Hollins, illustrated by Beth Webb. Designed to help people who become unwell and are diagnosed as having cancer. This book deals honestly with the unpleasant side of treatment, including chemotherapy and radiotherapy, and ends on a positive note.

Looking After my Heart (2005) by Sheila Hollins, Francesco Cappuccio and Paul Adeline, illustrated by Lisa Kopper. A book about Jane, who smokes and eats unhealthily and suffers a heart attack. After tests, she is given medication, changes her lifestyle, and recovers fully.

Sonia's Feeling Sad (2011) by Sheila Hollins and Roger Banks, illustrated by Lisa Kopper. Sonia is feeling so sad that she shuts herself off from her family and friends. She agrees to see a counsellor and gradually begins to feel better.

Ron's Feeling Blue (2011, 2nd edition) by Sheila Hollins, Roger Banks and Jenny Curran, illustrated by Beth Webb. When Ron retires to bed and shuns his friends, his GP arranges to see him regularly. She helps Ron to enjoy life again.

Books Beyond Words

A wide range of other titles is available in this series. See **www.booksbeyondwords.co.uk**

Authors

Sheila Hollins is Emeritus Professor of Psychiatry of Disability at St George's, University of London, and sits in the House of Lords. She is a past President and an Honorary Fellow of the Royal College of Psychiatrists. She is founding editor of Books Beyond Words and Executive Chair of Beyond Words.

Sandra Dowling is a Social Anthropologist who has been working in research in the field of learning and developmental disabilities for the past 15 years. She is a Research Fellow at Queen's University Belfast and a Honorary Research Fellow at the University of Ulster, NI. Her specialisms include identity, disabled childhoods, sports and social inclusion, as well as social and psychological well-being of people with intellectual disabilities, in particular, bereavement, loss and self-harming behaviour. She has published and presented her research widely.

Noëlle Blackman is CEO of Respond, a charity which provides psychotherapy to people with learning disabilities who have experienced abuse or trauma. She has co-facilitated the GOLD group since 1998.

Catherine Brighton was trained at Central Saint Martins College of Art and the Royal College of Art, and has written and illustrated many children's picture books and other titles in the Books Beyond Words series.

Acknowledgements

We would like to thank our editorial advisers, Pat Charlesworth, Nigel Hollins and the Women's Group at Blakes & Link Employment Agency, for helping us to think of ideas for this book and for telling us what was needed in the pictures. We would also like to thank all those bereavement counsellors and their clients in Merton, Wandsworth, Bognor, Edinburgh and Inverness who also had ideas about what was needed in the pictures.

We were very lucky to have representatives on the book's Advisory Group from Cruse Bereavement Care and St George's Hospital Medical School. We would like to thank Paul Adeline, Rosie Dalzell and Jane Hubert for their time which they gave most generously. Thanks also to Dorothea Duncan for her continuing commitment to the series.

Our grateful thanks go to roc and Hertfordshire Partnership NHS Trust for releasing Noëlle Blackman to work on this book as a co-author.

Finally, we are grateful to the Communities of L'Arche for their partnership in the Community Fund research project which helped to make this book possible.

Beyond Words: publications and training

Books Beyond Words will help family carers, support workers and professionals working with people who find pictures easier than words for understanding their world. A list of all Beyond Words publications, including Books Beyond Words titles, and where to buy them, can be found on our website:
www.booksbeyondwords.co.uk
email: **admin@booksbeyondwords.co.uk**

Workshops about using Books Beyond Words are provided regularly in London, or can be arranged in other localities on request. For information about forthcoming workshops see our website. Self-advocates are welcome.

Video clips showing our books being read are also on our website and YouTube channel:
www.youtube.com/user/booksbeyondwords and on our DVD, *How to Use Books Beyond Words*.

How to read 'When Somebody Dies'

There is no right or wrong way to read this book. Remember it is not necessary to be able to read the words.

1. Some people are not used to reading books. Start at the beginning and read the story in each picture.

2. Whether you are reading the book with one person or with a group, encourage them to tell the story in their own words. You will discover what each person thinks is happening, what they already know, and how they feel. You may think something different is happening in the pictures yourself, but that doesn't matter. Wait to see if their ideas change as the story develops. Don't challenge the reader(s) or suggest their ideas are wrong.

3. Some pictures may be more difficult to understand. It can help to prompt the people you are supporting, for example:

- Who do you think that is?
- What is happening?
- What is he or she doing now?
- How is he or she feeling?
- Do you feel like that? Has it happened to you/ your friend/ your family?

4. You don't have to read the whole book in one sitting. Allow people enough time to follow the pictures at their own pace.

5. Some people will not be able to follow the story, but they may be able to understand some of the pictures. Stay a little longer with the pictures that interest them.